FINDIN
WIT1

Justification Explained

Maurice Roberts

Therefore being justified by faith we have peace with God . . .
ROMANS 5:1

THE BANNER OF TRUTH TRUST

THE BANNER OF TRUTH TRUST
3 Murrayfield Road, Edinburgh EH12 6EL, UK
PO Box 621, Carlisle, PA 17013, USA

*

© The Banner of Truth Trust 2013

ISBN
Print: 978 1 84871 278 2
EPUB: 978 1 84871 279 9
Kindle: 978 1 84871 280 5

*

Typeset in 11/13 pt Adobe Garamond Pro
at the Banner of Truth Trust, Edinburgh

Printed in the USA by
Versa Press, Inc.,
East Peoria, IL

*To my sister Ann and her husband David
and to all their Family*

Contents

1. Our Relationship to God

AS soon as we start to read the Bible we begin to realise that the most important thing in life is our relationship to God. Until we are familiar with the Bible we do not pay attention to our need to be in a good relationship with God. A hundred other things take up our attention. Life keeps us very busy attending to these other things—our work, family, job, health, friends and interests. But scarcely a moment's time is given to the most vital question of all: *Am I in a right relationship with God?*

However, when we read the Bible with care and attention we begin to see more and more clearly that nothing matters so much as to be right with God. This very fact is the key to understanding our times and evaluating the society in which we live. When society is as it should be, people are concerned to know God. But when few are interested in knowing God, it is the proof that the society we live in is in a state of decay.

As soon as we think of having a relationship with God we know instinctively that it has something to do with how we live our lives and how we behave. The more we know the teaching of the Bible the more clearly we see that God looks not only at our outward behaviour but also at our secret thoughts and at our inner motives and desires. To all of us this discovery is an uncomfortable one. For we all know, if we are honest with ourselves, that there are dark and unpleasant things in our hearts and minds which ought not to be there. If God sees all our secrets then we have reason to be concerned—even alarmed.

Those who do not read the Bible may be more or less ignorant of this uncomfortable fear which Bible-readers have. They will probably say that they do not believe in any sort of God and they are happy to have no fears on account of their private thoughts, words or deeds.

However, strange as this may seem to those who do not know

what God tells us in the Bible, it is a much safer and healthier thing to have a troubled conscience on account of our inner guilt than to be free from all anxiety or fear at the thought of being guilty before God. The reason is this: a sense of guilt before God will tend to drive us to look for a remedy for our spiritual condition. On the other hand, if we are happy not to know or feel our guilt we are unlikely to want to go to God to find the real cure for it.

Jesus Christ uses a famous illustration to explain this point. He says that a man who is well does not need a doctor. It is the man who knows he is sick who welcomes a doctor (*Mark* 2:17). There is more to this illustration than one might think on first reading it. Christ knew what lies in men's hearts. His meaning is that a person may be seriously ill and not know it. A man may be deluded into thinking he is well when really he is ill. But, on the other hand, a man who knows and feels his illness will welcome the doctor's advice and accept his treatment.

Christ is here not concerned with physical but with moral and spiritual illness. In other words, Christ is here speaking about a man's relationship to God. If we are unconcerned about it, we shall not welcome help and healing. But if we have a sense of guilt and fear that our relationship with God is wrong, we shall be grateful for someone to bring us the medicine we inwardly know we need.

The fact is, as the Bible tells us over and over again, we are all of us in need of being put right in our relationship to God. This is a very humbling piece of information. But it is essential for us to grasp if we are to become right with God. For we are all born with an evil nature which we cannot put right. We are all sinful and guilty, even from our mother's womb.

The Bible has been given to mankind by God as the explanation of how we have all gone wrong and—mercifully—how God can put us right and bring us into a new relationship with himself in which we are no longer regarded by him as guilty and worthy of punishment. This is why the Bible needs to be read and studied carefully. It is an inspired record of what is wrong with us all and an inspiring account of how God has taken steps to have us healed and restored to his favour.

But we must at this point pause to ask an obvious question: If the Bible is so important and helpful to people, why do not more people read it? Several things could be said in answer to this question.

For one thing, the Bible has been avidly read and studied in some generations. Millions of people in the past have had their lives transformed for the better by it. This is especially true of people in the past who lived in Britain, Europe and America. Then too, we need to appreciate that today in the countries of Asia and Africa millions of people are now reading the Bible in their own languages and are coming to know how to get right with God.

If the further question be asked: Why are not more people in the West reading the Bible today? the answer is: Because they do not realise how extremely important it is to get right with God. People are too much caught up with minor problems to pay attention to the supremely important problem in life.

Problems are of various kinds. There are less serious problems, more serious problems and extremely serious problems. For example, to have a heavy cold is only a minor problem. But to lose your sight and to become blind is a major problem. However, more serious still is to develop untreatable cancer. The former problems are less serious than the latter. Everyone knows that this is so.

Apply this principle to the subject in hand and it means this. Most people are so caught up with life's lesser problems that they do not take the time or the trouble to consider what is the most serious problem of all in life. Matters of health, housing, jobs and family are of far less seriousness than that of living and dying in a wrong relationship to God.

Does that sound surprising? Do you ask why that should be? Do you perhaps say that 'God is love' and so all will be well in the end? It is gloriously and wonderfully true that 'God is love.' The Bible tells us so again and again. But the Bible also tells us that 'God is light' and that therefore God will punish the guilty and all those who die without making their peace with him. God is infinitely holy and just.

The very clear teaching of the Bible is that the only time we have to get into a right relationship with God is our brief life-span in this present world. Once we are dead the window of opportunity to get right with God is over and gone forever. Does that much matter? Emphatically, *YES!* Because if a person dies in a wrong relationship with God he, or she, will go into a condition of eternal punishment.

On the other hand, if in this life we make our peace with God we shall at death enter into heaven, peace and everlasting life.

Surprising as it may seem, the best thing that can happen to anyone in this life is to become seriously concerned about their guiltiness before God. To become aware of our spiritual sickness and our guilt is the first step in seeking the spiritual Doctor, Jesus Christ, and taking the medicine which he has prescribed for all who want to become right with God.

Sadly, many who are told of their need to go to Christ for the sake of their souls turn away from him and go back to the vain pleasures of life. Either they think it is too much trouble to read the Bible and pray to God for his help and grace, or else they prefer to stifle their sense of guilt and choose to live without God, as so many people, sadly, choose to do.

But there is a very serious reason why we should never postpone the call to seek God and find our peace with him. It is because turning our back on God is a form of spiritual suicide.

If we seek him with all our heart we shall certainly find him. This is what God has promised to us all. But if we despise the call of God to seek him we shall incur his displeasure. If we offend God he may cease to strive with us. He may allow us to go on and on in life till at last we meet him as our Judge in death and at the Judgment Day. If we die without being reconciled to God it would be better if we had never been born.

2. Our Need of Justification

THE Bible, like all important books, contains technical terms which we need to have explained to us. Whatever field of study we enter there are technical terms to be learned. Whether a person studies to be a doctor, or a scientist, or a politician, he or she must know what the technical terms in his or her field of study mean. So it is in matters of Christian faith.

We refer to these main points as the *doctrines* of the Christian religion. We have in mind by this term such vital truths as the following: God the Trinity, the Incarnation of Christ, the Atonement made by Christ on the cross, Justification and Sanctification.

There are many other doctrines besides these. But these are examples of what we mean by the doctrines. They are the great points of teaching relating to the faith of Christ and his church. Such doctrines may be thought of as the essential technical terms of the Christian religion. They are needed in order to make clear to all what God has revealed to us in the Bible and what, therefore, we are to believe if we are to be brought into a right relationship with God.

Our concern now is with the doctrine of *Justification*. This may be compared to the door into the Christian faith. Justification deals with the extremely important subject of man's coming into a right relationship to God, who is our Maker and our Judge. To understand what God in the Bible teaches concerning justification is all-important to a person who is seeking to get into a right relationship with God.

This is all the more so because the way in which sinners may get right with God is very different from what might be expected. Thousands of persons have gone wrong at this crucially important point. They have followed the wrong path and sadly failed to find true peace with God. We dare not therefore trust our own wisdom in the matter of how we may become justified with God. The only right way to go is to keep to the way of justification which God himself has revealed to us in the Bible, which is his revelation to man.

Let us look first at some of the wrong and false ways of finding acceptance and favour with God.

A very common mistake is to suppose that we can balance our good works against our bad works and in that way gain God's favour. The idea is this: People who do not know their Bible suppose that they have good deeds and bad deeds, good works and bad works, good thoughts and bad thoughts. Well then, they say, the way to get God's pardon and blessing is to do some good things to balance out the bad things.

The 'good things' which they have in mind are such things as these: giving money to the poor; going occasionally to church; saying a prayer; doing someone else a good turn. To use a common expression, they seek to do their 'good deed for the day'. Their hope and expectation commonly is that in these ways they will please God and, in the end, will have done enough good deeds to balance out all their bad deeds, such as telling lies, swearing, stealing, *etc*.

The general idea is that God will reckon up the 'good deeds' and allow them into heaven on the grounds of their being, on the whole, rather more 'good' than bad. The balance, so to say, is just a little in their favour. Their virtues make up just over fifty per cent and so, on that basis, they hope to come off well when they meet God in the Judgment.

What is wrong with this way of looking to have God's favour and forgiveness? It is a mistake which has two glaring weaknesses which must be pointed out. First, until we are justified and in a right relationship with God we are entirely incapable of doing any 'good work'. In God's eyes, a 'good work' is something which can only be done by a 'good person'; that is, by someone who is justified, pardoned and right with God. So, till we, as persons, are right in God's sight, nothing we do is 'good'. Even our best works are 'filthy rags' in the sight of a holy God. To use a Bible illustration, the tree must be made good before its fruit can be good (*Matt.* 7:17-20). So, till a man or a woman is good in God's judgment, all that he or she does is worthless as a means of gaining God's favour or getting us into a right relationship with God. This is one very important aspect of the problem of balancing our evil with our good works.

But there is a second great problem. It is that fifty-one per cent of goodness will not make us good enough for heaven. God created man perfect in the beginning. Adam and Eve were 100 per cent righteous as God originally created them. We now are sinners because Adam disobeyed God and ruined the human race. But God still requires us all to be 100 per cent righteous if we, in our own day and age, are to get to heaven at last. So, the problem of getting right with God cannot possibly be solved by our attempting to become good enough for God by what we may fancy to be our 'good works'.

But there is a more elaborate idea in the world for getting to heaven which is also completely wrong. It is the idea invented by men that the church can prepare us to be right with God.

The idea goes like this: If I devote myself to prayer and become a monk or a nun; if I am very diligent in confessing my sins to a minister of the church; if I am regular in taking the sacrament of the Lord's supper; if I am baptized; if I mortify myself and spend hours in fasting and devotional exercises, I shall be good enough for God and so get to heaven at last.

Now all this is very impressive. It does not appeal to everybody but it has always had an appeal for some men and women. They devote their entire life to religious exercises and devotions in the hope that if they do all this they will be right with God and be allowed at last into the glory of heaven.

What are we to think of this approach to getting into a right relationship with God? It is completely mistaken and worthless. Nowhere does God tell us in the Bible that we shall be justified and pardoned on the basis of our devotions, prayers, fastings or our diligent use of the sacraments of baptism and the Lord's supper.

The basic and fundamental mistakes here are the same as before. First, our 'good works' done before we are reconciled to God have neither merit nor virtue in the sight of God. Till we are justified we are incapable of any 'good work', though we were to pray and fast for twelve hours every day. Since 'good works' done before justification cannot justify us, they are worthless as a way of putting us into a right relationship with God.

Also, as we saw before, any attempt to obtain a justification which is not 100 per cent righteous in the sight of God is hopelessly incapable of placing us in a right relationship with God as our Judge.

The humbling truth is that mankind is so ruined by the fall of Adam that no amount of 'good works' done by us before we are justified can give us either God's pardon or his allowance to enter heaven.

What we have said above is all bad news to those who imagine they can by their own religious efforts patch up the very serious situation in which all of us are born; that is, of not being right with God.

However, the pathway to an understanding of the right way to please God begins by first knowing what are the wrong ways. The subject is a very serious and important one. Indeed, it is the most important subject of all as it concerns our salvation and our spiritual wellbeing both in this life and the next. Jesus Christ makes this clear so often in his teaching and preaching. His way of directing men's thoughts to this vital subject of salvation is summed up like this: 'For what shall it profit a man, if he shall gain the whole world, and lose his own soul? Or what shall a man give in exchange for his soul?' (*Mark* 8:36-37).

God, in his mercy, has not left us all in the dark as to what we must do to get right with him. But we shall not benefit from his teaching unless we set our minds to seek after the way of life which he teaches. The subject is that of man's justification. How can we get it? We confess that there are wrong and false ways of being reconciled to God. But what then is the true way?

3. God's Gift of Righteousness

THE wonderful truth that lies at the heart of the Christian gospel is that the righteousness which mankind needs, and which no man can attain to by his own efforts, has been provided for us by God himself. Since mankind is sinful, lost and ruined, God, in his great love, has done all that is needed to provide for us the gift of righteousness so that we may be justified.

The steps which God has taken to give us a free gift of righteousness are wonderful and glorious. To appreciate God's wonderful gift we must know that God is a Trinity. That is to say, there are three Persons in the one Godhead: the Father, the Son and the Holy Spirit. Each Person is fully God. All three Persons are equal. Each Person is holy, perfect and divine. Each Person is infinite, eternal and unchangeable.

In order to give to sinful men and women the righteousness we need to be justified, God the Father sent his Son into this world. By this we mean that Jesus Christ, God's Son, took our human nature into union with himself. We refer to this as the Incarnation. Jesus, after the Incarnation, now had two natures. He was both God and Man in two natures, yet as one Person. No other being has ever been like Christ. We refer to him as the God-Man.

The reason why Christ took a human nature into union with his divine nature is so that he might be our Representative. He came so as to live for us and die for us. His work involved him in perfectly keeping all the commandments of God.

The Bible makes it clear that he was born of a virgin and so had a miraculous birth. The reason for his virgin birth was to give to Jesus Christ a perfect, sinless human nature. Had Christ been born as we are, he would have been a sinner as we are. To put it technically, we may say that sin would have defiled the Person of Christ in two ways. First, he would have had the sin of our first father Adam imputed to him. Second, he would have inherited a sinful, fallen nature from his parents.

If Jesus Christ had been sinful at his birth, as we are, he could never have been our Saviour. He could not have given to us what we need to have given to us—a *perfect righteousness*. But since our Lord Jesus Christ was spotless and holy he was able perfectly to keep the Ten Commandments, which are the Moral Law of God, and to live an entire life on earth in which there was not the least degree of sin, disobedience or fault in the judgment of God the Father.

Still more, Jesus Christ, being appointed by God the Father to be the Saviour of fallen sinners, was able to take our place and to suffer in our room and stead. This he did upon the cross, on which he died for us, taking upon himself our guilt and paying by his agony and his sufferings the debt which we owe to God's justice because of our sins.

It is necessary to use one or two rather technical words in order to bring out the meaning and importance of what Christ did by his perfect life and his death on the cross. We say that his life and death were *vicarious*. By that we mean that he lived and died for us. By this means Christ can save, cleanse and justify us. This is so because God the Father is willing to accept what our Lord did as a thing done for us. Christ's life of perfect obedience can be reckoned as valid for us. His vicarious death on the cross can be reckoned as payment to God the Father for our disobedience.

In explaining this wonderful doctrine we use the term *imputation*. We say that our sins were imputed to Christ and that his obedience is imputed to us. We may say that Christ has done for us what we could not do for ourselves and what no one else could do for us. He has provided for us a righteousness by which we may be justified in the sight of God. No wonder the Bible tells us in the light of this that 'God so loved the world that he gave his only begotten Son that whosoever believeth in him should not perish but have everlasting life' (*John* 3:16)!

There is no book in all the world which tells us so wonderful a message as this gospel, which is in the Bible. It is so simple, so sweet and so much what we need. The great gospel is just this: that what we could not do to make ourselves acceptable to God, Christ has done by living and dying for us.

It is for this reason that we say that Jesus Christ is 'the Lord our Righteousness'. He is called the 'Lamb of God which takes away the sin of the world' (*John* 1:29). Christ is said to 'wash us from our sins in his own blood' (*Rev.* 1:5). Again, the Bible says about Christ that he 'was made sin for us that we might be made the righteousness of God in him' (*2 Cor.* 5:21). In a word, we are taught by these expressions that Jesus Christ has done exactly what we needed to have done for us: he has provided the way for sinners to be justified before God.

It is for this reason that we refer to the message of salvation by Christ as the *gospel*. The word means 'good news', and good news the gospel certainly is. It informs us that God, who is most righteous and cannot overlook sin, has provided a means by which sin can be pardoned and sinners enter at last into heaven.

We need to remind ourselves of the terrible truth that if Christ had not died for us there would be no way in which we could be justified. If the question therefore is asked, Why does God not just pardon everyone's sin and admit them all to heaven?, the answer we give is this: God will forgive no sin unless his justice receives satisfaction. God, in other words, requires that all sin be punished with the degree of punishment that fits that sin. That is what all justice demands. God explicitly informs us that he 'will by no means clear the guilty' (*Exod.* 34:7). God hates all sin. Because of his perfect justice he must and will punish it. But there is a wonderful provision made for us in the life and death of Christ. If we want to be forgiven, for Christ's sake we may be.

In the next chapter we shall look at the important question of how we may receive the justification and free forgiveness which Christ has purchased for us at so great a cost. Before we come to that, however, it is important to understand what is the price to pay for ignoring or despising what the Lord Jesus Christ has done. Salvation is not something that people get automatically. It is not given to any who do not seek it with all their heart and pray to God to give it to them.

If we treat this gospel lightly we shall be guilty of offending God. It would be better to live and die never having heard this gospel of God's grace than to know it and not to value it very highly. There are still places on earth where the gospel is scarcely known—or even not known at all. In the case of such poor souls it is impossible for them to be saved from their sin. They do not know what Christ has done and so they cannot benefit from it. This is why missionaries have gone out from this and other lands to preach and teach the ignorant of all nations, as Christ commanded his people to do (*Matt.* 28:19-20). If people do not know the gospel they will not benefit from it. They must die in their sins and suffer forever the punishment due to their disobedience to God's Moral Law while they lived in this world.

But, terrible as this is, there is something still more fearful. It is to live in a country where the gospel of Christ is known and where Bibles are to be had easily—and yet, in spite of these privileges, to treat the salvation which Christ has obtained for us with contempt. The way the Bible puts it is very clear: 'How shall we escape if we neglect so great salvation?' (*Heb.* 2:3).

There is a most important principle to be seen here: The greater our privilege in the things of God, the greater our guilt if we do not make use of our privilege. Jesus Christ tells us something which might well make us shiver with fear. He tells some who heard and saw him, but who rejected his gospel, that it would be more tolerable in the Day of Judgment for the wicked nations of the Old Testament, called Sodom and Gomorrah, than for them (*Matt.* 10:15). It is a fearful thing to treat the gospel carelessly.

4. Salvation by Faith Alone

GOD has appointed and ordered every aspect of the gospel in the wisest and best way. Our duty as sinful men and women is to do what God commands. The Bible is God's revelation of the truth and is relevant to every aspect of our life and the salvation of which it speaks: Creation, Protection, Justification and Judgment.

So long as we go by the teaching of the Bible we shall be safe. But history and experience teach us that people are prone to slipping away from the clear teaching of the Bible and mixing Bible teaching with human speculation or else human tradition. As soon as we do this we go wrong.

Let us apply this principle to the matter of man's justification before God. How, we must ask, does any person receive the righteousness which Christ by his life and death came to earth to purchase for lost sinners? Do we get this righteousness as a reward for our devotions, prayers and other 'good works'? Are we given it when we are baptized or else when we become members of a church? Do we become righteous as a result of eating the bread and drinking the wine in the sacrament of the Lord's supper? In any case, who pronounces a sinner to be justified? Is it the minister, or the bishop, or the Pope?

These are all questions which men in the past have often gone wrong about. But, bearing in mind the extreme importance of them, these questions are matters upon which we must be absolutely clear. So long as we keep to the teaching of the Bible we shall not go wrong.

A sinner is justified as soon as he, or she, believes in the Lord Jesus Christ. God pronounces us righteous immediately the instant we place our trust in Christ as the Saviour whom God sent into the world to live and die for us. There is no place whatever in justification for the merit, so-called, of our own good works. Neither the sacraments, nor prayers, nor devotions, nor good works of any kind enter into a sinner's justification before God.

This is the clear teaching of the Bible and it is essential that we do not allow any false teaching to spoil our understanding. The great Apostle Paul states: 'Therefore we conclude that a man is justified by faith without the deeds of the law' (*Rom.* 3:28). We see from these words that nothing but faith justifies us. By 'works of the law' Paul means our observance of the Moral Law, the Ten Commandments. The Ten Commandments cannot save us. Our own good works cannot justify us, either in whole or in part.

Again Paul states: 'For by grace are ye saved through faith: and that not of yourselves: it is the gift of God: not of works, lest any man should boast' (*Eph.* 2:8-9). By the word 'grace' Paul means that the method by which sinners are saved has been appointed and provided by God in his great love and pity for us in our fallen and our lost condition. In words which are unmistakably clear, Paul states that we are justified and saved by God by faith alone and without works of any kind on our part. In a word, we are justified only by faith in Christ.

This teaching of Paul is exactly the same as that of Christ himself. 'Thy faith hath saved thee; go in peace', says Christ to the penitent woman who came into Simon the Pharisee's house (*Luke* 7:50). 'Today shalt thou be with me in paradise', says Christ to the dying thief who prayed to him (*Luke* 23:43). 'Dost thou believe on the Son of God?' asks Christ of the blind man as he gives him spiritual sight (*John* 9:35).

The method of salvation is always the same. When any sinner gets pardon and salvation it is in this way and in no other. It is when he, or she, believes in Jesus as the eternal Son of God. So Peter can write of Christians that they are 'kept by the power of God through faith unto salvation' (*1 Pet.* 1:5). No wonder then that Paul states the matter of our salvation in these words: 'After that the kindness and love of God our Saviour toward man appeared, not by works of righteousness which we have done, but according to his mercy he saved us, . . . that being justified by his grace, we should be made heirs according to the hope of eternal life' (*Titus* 3:4-7).

We are saved and justified, then, not by our own 'good works' but by faith in Jesus Christ. Why should this be so? We have to admit that to be saved by faith is very much contrary to what we might expect. Does God not ask of us to contribute in some way towards our justification and salvation? To get the forgiveness of sins and promise of eternal life absolutely free and without any contribution from us seems to be just too good. Can we not pay back at least some of our debt to God's justice? Must we have Christ to pay for all our vile sins without at least some small share of merit contributed by ourselves?

The reasons why God will not permit the sinner to make any contribution towards his own justification are made clear to us in the Bible. For one thing, there is nothing left for us to pay! Christ has by his precious blood paid our debt to God's justice in full. This is implied in Christ's glorious cry just before he died on the cross: 'It is finished!' (*John* 19:30). The words convey the wonderful truth that Jesus has paid every last penny of our debt.

Our poor human efforts are in any case so imperfect. Our feeble efforts at 'doing good'—by prayers, or fasting, or acts of charity . . . How good to know that God is perfectly satisfied with what Christ has done! My feeble acts of devotion cannot add to the sublime perfections of his death! If *Christ* died for me I am sure of a perfect pardon. To pretend to add to his work is more than laughable. What good deeds of a ruined sinner like me are fit to be added as a supplement to the transcendentally great act of sacrifice made by the incarnate Son of God? 'It is finished!' cried Christ. We have nothing to do but to believe and rest upon his perfect sacrifice. In him every believing sinner finds rest and peace.

There is another reason why God will not allow us to think of adding our own 'merits' to Christ's in the matter of our justification. 'Not of works, lest any man should boast' (*Eph.* 2:9). So declares the inspired Apostle Paul. The fact is here implied that if we were invited to add our own merits to those of Christ we should boast of being partly our own saviours! So corrupt is the human heart! Therefore God will not allow human merits of any kind to play any part whatsoever in our salvation.

One of the great tragedies of the Christian church during the Middle Ages is that this doctrine of justification by faith alone in Christ alone became buried under a mountain of man-made church traditions. Thanks to God, this biblical doctrine of justification by faith without works was rescued at the time of the great Protestant Reformation.

It was not a new doctrine invented by Martin Luther which emerged at the Reformation. It was the rediscovery of what the Bible everywhere teaches. What happened at the Reformation was the removal of the centuries of moss and lichen from the noble monument of the New Testament doctrine of justification. Martin Luther's protest led to the reaffirmation of what had been preached and taught for centuries in the early Christian church.

Justification by faith is the only way a sinner may come to have a right relationship with God. Happy and blessed indeed is every man, woman or child who lays aside all hope of salvation by prayers, sacraments or church traditions and casts his, or her, soul at the foot of the cross as the only hope of having the loving pardon of Almighty God!

So the New Testament gospel is just this: 'Believe on the Lord Jesus Christ, and thou shalt be saved' (*Acts* 16:31). When a sinner believes in Jesus a number of wonderful things happen to him. God, as the great Judge, pronounces from heaven that he is righteous, being now clothed in the imputed righteousness of Christ. All his sins—past, present and to come—are pardoned. He passes from a state of sin to a state of grace, being now in Christ and united to Christ.

One caution needs to be made at this point. There is such a thing as false, or counterfeit, faith. Such 'faith' is seen in hypocrites such as Judas Iscariot, who betrayed Christ with a kiss. The Epistle of James warns us that the faith we need for justification must be real and not spurious. The way to know if a person's faith is real or not is to take account of how they live and behave.

James cites the cases of Abraham and Rahab to show that those whose faith is genuine will show it by their good works. Whilst good works do not justify us before God, who can read men's hearts, they do justify us before our fellow-men.

Our good works show that our faith, by which we are justified before God, is that real faith which God has commanded us to exercise in his gospel (*James* 2:19-26). Worthless 'faith' makes us no better than the 'devils' (*James* 2:19).

The way to think of it is this:

- The MERIT of our justification is Christ's obedience.
- The MEANS of our receiving it is faith alone.
- The MARK of true faith is godly behaviour.

So, when a person is justified he, or she, shows it by a life of grateful obedience to the God who has pardoned them.

5. The Teaching on Justification in the Early Church

IT is important to be clear on the point made earlier that justification by faith alone in Christ was the teaching of the Early Church. We commonly refer to these early Christian writers as the 'Church Fathers'. By this term we do not, and should not, imply that they were the authority on whose teaching we must rely for our knowledge of doctrine. That was by no means their view of themselves. They sought to draw their teaching from a careful study of the Bible as the inspired Word of God, as we today should seek to do.

The value of knowing what the Church Fathers taught about justification lies in this: that we are able today to compare it with the teaching of the great Protestant Reformers like Luther and Calvin. As a consequence we are better placed to know whether what these Reformers wrote was completely new, as the Church of Rome tends to assert, or whether the Reformers were only referring to the original view of justification found in the Early Church writers.

A caution, which we must always keep in mind when looking

at the views of these early Christian writers, is that they did not always express themselves correctly on every point of doctrine. Furthermore, they did not always agree with one another on all points of doctrine. Consequently we do not study the Church Fathers in order to prove or disprove what the Reformers taught, but only to discover if, on the doctrine of justification, they taught substantially and essentially the same thing. The great point for us to notice is whether these Early Church writers taught that we are justified by faith alone, or that to faith must be added 'good works' of our own. In this way, we may benefit from looking at a few of the statements made by respected theologians in the Early Church. Here are some helpful quotations for us to use in assessing if our post-Reformation doctrine is completely new, or whether it is only a re-statement of the Church Fathers:

IRENAEUS

'As through the disobedience of one man many were made sinners, and forfeited life, so it behoved also, that through the obedience of one man who first was born from the Virgin, many should be justified, and receive salvation.'[1] Again he says: 'But now, without the Law, the righteousness of God is manifested, being witnessed by the Law and the Prophets; for "the just shall live by faith". But that "the just shall live by faith", had been foretold by the Prophets.'

It should be noted here that the emphasis in justification is placed on these three things: (1) the obedience of Christ; (2) faith on the part of those who enjoy the justification which Christ, by his obedience, has provided for sinners; (3) Justification is affirmed to be 'without the Law', that is, without the need on our part to attempt to do any 'good works'.

---

[1] James Buchanan, *The Doctrine of Justification*, (Edinburgh: Banner of Truth Trust, 1984), pp. 107-10.

24

CYPRIAN

'What person was more a priest of the Most High God than our Lord Jesus Christ, who offered a sacrifice unto God the Father? ... If Abraham "believed in God, and it was imputed unto him for righteousness", then each one who believes in God, and lives by faith, is found to be a righteous person, and long since, in faithful Abraham, is shown to be blessed and justified.'

The points to note with special care here are: (1) The action of Christ in his offering up of himself as a sacrifice to God in what provides the propitiation for our sins; (2) Righteousness comes, whether to Abraham or to anyone else, by faith; (3) This righteousness is that of Christ and it comes to sinners by imputation when we believe the gospel.

ATHANASIUS

'Not by these [*i.e.,* our works] but by faith, a man is justified as was Abraham.'

We note that all human works are here excluded and that justification comes to sinners by faith. The reference here to Abraham refers to the argument made by Paul in such passages of the New Testament as Romans 4 and Galatians 3.

BASIL

'This is the true and perfect glorying in God, when a man is not lifted up on account of his own righteousness, but has known himself to be wanting in true righteousness, and to be justified by faith alone in Christ.'

We must note with special attention that this early writer uses the phrase 'justified by faith alone in Christ'. This is precisely the view which Luther and all the other Reformers came to hold in the sixteenth century. It is obvious that they did not invent this view but simply affirmed what they had found in the Church Fathers. In turn the Church Fathers used the phrase 'by faith alone in Christ' because they were convinced it reflects the teaching of the Bible.

AMBROSE

'Without the works of the Law, to an ungodly man, that is to say a Gentile, believing in Christ, his "faith is imputed for righteousness" as also it was to Abraham.'

Ambrose goes on to ask how the Jews could imagine there is justification through the works of the Law. His own conclusion on this subject is summed up in these clear words: 'There is no need therefore of the Law, since through faith alone an ungodly man is justified with God.'

We must note this plain and clear explanation of how justification takes place in a person's life. It is, he affirms, 'through faith alone'. This biblical view of the doctrine of justification is exactly what the Reformers reaffirmed at a later date.

ORIGEN

'Through faith, without the works of the Law, the thief was justified; because, for that purpose, the Lord inquired not what he had previously wrought, nor yet waited for his performance of some work after he should have believed; but, when about to enter into paradise, he took him unto himself for a companion, justified through his confession alone.'

Again, in the above words we see how clearly these early Christian writers were convinced in their own mind that justification is, as Origen states it, 'through faith, without the works of the Law'. To say here that the thief on the cross was 'justified through his confession alone' is simply another way of saying that he was justified on the basis of faith in Christ, a faith which manifested itself in this dying man's confession.

JEROME

'When an ungodly man is converted, God justifies him through faith alone, not on account of good works, which he possessed not; otherwise, on account of his ungodly deeds, he ought to have been punished.'

Jerome, the translator of the Bible into Latin, known as the Vulgate, which was used for a thousand years in the Western Church, certainly did not believe or teach that human works need to be added to faith in order for sinners to receive justification and eternal life from God. Rather, the tragic truth is that in the Middle Ages the biblical doctrine of justification by faith alone without works was lost and for many centuries buried until it was rediscovered in the Bible by the Reformers.

CHRYSOSTOM

'What then did God do? . . . "He made . . . a righteous person to be a sinner, in order that he might make sinners righteous" . . . not simply that we might be made righteous, but that we might be made the very "righteousness of God".'

So, Chrysostom's doctrine of justification is that it comes to us wholly and only by the imputation of sin to Christ and the counter-imputation of Christ's righteousness to us. 'Good works' done by the sinner are a thousand miles away from the mind of this worthy Church Father.

AUGUSTINE

'All who are justified through Christ, are righteous, not in themselves, but in him.'

When Augustine here declares that believers are not righteous 'in themselves' he clearly means that no 'good works' which we can do have any place whatsoever in a sinner's justification before God.

The above quotations help us to see that the great teachers of the Early Church taught what the Reformers taught after the Middle Ages.

6. Errors and Falsehoods to be Avoided

THE history of the church of Christ teaches us all many lessons. One such lesson is that error and falsehood may creep into the thinking of churches and theologians over a period of time. There are a variety of reasons for this.

Churches may lose sight of the great first principle in the formulation of doctrine, that the quarry from which all sound doctrine must be drawn is the Bible. The religion of Christ is one given by divine revelation. This was Christ's own method. The solution to questions of doctrine and practice were resolved by Christ in a simple appeal to Scripture: 'What is written?' Similarly, the apostles, as inspired men, taught that 'all scripture is given by inspiration of God' (*2 Tim.* 3:16) and that the Bible is a 'light that shineth in a dark place' (*2 Pet.* 1:19).

Christ makes it clear that church tradition is an invalid source of information when it is used to formulate doctrine or right practice (*Matt.* 15:3-9). He explicitly warns against 'the leaven of the Pharisees and of the Sadducees' (*Matt.* 16:6).

The 'leaven of the Pharisees' was the practice of adding traditions to the Bible. The 'leaven of the Sadducees' on the other hand was the tendency to remove and ignore some of the inspired books of the Bible. Our rule in matters of doctrine and practice ought to be to use the Bible, the whole Bible, and nothing but the Bible, as the source of information for the formulation of all our doctrines and practices.

The Bible itself ends with this very solemn warning: 'If any man shall add unto these things, God shall add unto him the plagues that are written in this book: And if any man shall take away from the words of the book of this prophecy, God shall take away his part out of the book of life' (*Rev.* 22:18-19).

However, in spite of such warnings as these, men have drifted into serious error. Truth has on occasion been lost, falsehood has been given the official support of the church, and the man in the pew has been left with a spurious gospel which is nothing but a contradiction of God's Word.

The above observations are true with regard to many of the teachings of the Christian faith, but especially in the matter of man's justification before God. The long period of the Middle Ages witnessed a profound decline in the understanding of Christian doctrine and duty. At the root of this problem was ignorance of the Bible and the consequent promotion of human wisdom in the formulation of the way of salvation.

The way back from this era of darkness came only as men again had access to the Bible and the divine enlightenment which only those have who have been truly 'born again' of God's Holy Spirit. Till a church leader, be he theologian, bishop or preacher, has had the experience of the new birth he 'cannot see' the things which belong to God's spiritual kingdom (*John* 3:3).

In the light of the above sobering facts of church history it is not surprising to learn that in framing the doctrine of justification men have sometimes gone far away from the true teaching of God's Word. Tragically, this is true of the official teaching of the Roman Catholic Church in its doctrine of justification. The following quotations taken from the *Catechism of the Catholic Church* (1996) show that the Bible's teaching on this doctrine has not been followed:

> Justification is not only the remission of sins, but also the sanctification and renewal of the interior man (Part Three; 1427).

> Justification is conferred in Baptism, the sacrament of faith. It conforms us to the righteousness of God, who makes us inwardly just by the power of his mercy (Part Three; 1266).

The above teaching departs from the Bible at two points. First, it confuses justification with sanctification. Secondly, it makes baptism the means of justification. The Bible teaches neither of these doctrines. Sanctification is the work of God's Holy Spirit by which he purifies the heart of a sinner. Justification, on the other hand, refers to God's gracious act in imputing the righteousness of Christ to one who believes the gospel. The difference is a very important one and may be explained by a simple illustration.

In his gracious work of sanctification God acts as a doctor to cure the moral disease of a person's heart, or soul. But in his act of justification God acts as a judge in his great High Court of Justice and he pronounces the sentence of 'Not guilty' on the life and conduct of a sinner who believes in Jesus. These two spheres of divine activity are both involved in the salvation of the soul. But each is distinct and must be kept distinct in our definition of Christian doctrine; otherwise sinners will be misled on the vital matter of salvation.

The most serious error we can fall into when preaching the gospel is to point sinners in the wrong direction as to how they may be saved. The Apostle Paul states with the utmost vehemence: 'Though we, or an angel from heaven, preach any other gospel unto you than that which we have preached unto you, let him be accursed' (*Gal.* 1:8). He states this twice over: 'Let him be accursed' (*Gal.* 1:9).

The error which he condemns so vehemently here is altering the gospel. That means to misstate the conditions which a sinner must comply with to find forgiveness with God and eternal life. Paul expounds the doctrine of justification in great detail in his epistles, especially in Romans and Galatians. Nowhere does he, or any other apostle, teach that a sinner needs baptism as the vital condition for salvation. What the sinner *does* need is faith in Christ. Baptism has its place, but it is in no way the vital condition for justification.

If we tell the seeking sinner that he will be safe from God's condemnation if he is baptized, we are deceiving him and leading him into a dangerously false sense of security. Faith and baptism, after all, are by no means one and the same thing.

In the last few years a new error has become popularised which in a rather different way alters the biblical doctrine of justification. We refer to it as the New Perspective on Paul. It is the view that Paul in his epistles was not condemning the Jewish rabbinical doctrine of justification for being self-righteous. Rather, say its promoters, the rabbis were guilty of glorying in their 'Jewishness'. Their sin, it is said by these scholars, was not to boast of their own self-righteousness but rather to boast of their 'national righteousness' as Jews. This new view is that 'righteousness' means to be in a right 'covenant-relationship' with God.

The fault here is much the same. It is an alteration of the categories given by inspiration in the Bible. Justification in the Bible means to place a sinner into the condition of being freed from his guilt by the imputation to him of the righteousness of Christ. We may not alter the category of the law-court into that of covenant. Self-righteousness was unquestionably the sin of the Jewish Pharisees. The evidence for this is seen clearly in the parable of Christ in which the Pharisee thanks God that he is 'not as other men' (*Luke* 18:10-14). He boasts here not of his nationality but of his own 'good works'.

The Apostle Paul himself was once guilty of this self-righteousness. He was delivered from it when he came into a deep conviction, as a Pharisee, of his own inward corruption, notwithstanding his external conformity to God's law. His conversion was the sequel to his humbling self-knowledge (*Rom.* 7:7-13). Paul was deeply aware of how blind he himself had been before his conversion to Christ on the road to Damascus (*Acts* 9).

The concern which Paul had in warning us of false gospels arose in good measure from his own experience therefore. He had once been profoundly deceived as to his own good standing before God. He was now, after his conversion, deeply concerned lest others should be deceived as to their relationship to God (*Phil.* 3:1-10).

No folly is greater than to suppose ourselves right before God when we are not right before God. That had been Paul's experience. At the time of the Reformation Martin Luther's experience was somewhat similar. However, mercifully God kept alive his consciousness of sin until, by God's grace, he came to understand that God imputes righteousness to us by faith alone and without any 'good works' on our part. This is the sound doctrine we must keep to.

7. The Classic Statement

THE 'Golden Age' of theology in Britain was the seventeenth century. The Reformers had laid the foundations of biblical doctrine and had gone to their eternal rest. The generations that followed in England and Scotland now set about the task of refining these doctrinal statements and giving them their classic formulations.

Our forefathers at that date produced a good number of Catechisms and Confessional summaries which have been of great help to the churches over the centuries. None of these classic theological statements is more deserving of our respect than the Westminster Confession of Faith. The Chapter 'Of Justification' is an exemplary exposition of this cardinal doctrine. It is summarised here.

The first concern of those who composed this chapter on justification was to define it with precision and to ensure that it conformed at every point with the teaching of the Word of God. They lay out first of all the nature of justification.

Justification does not consist in 'infusing righteousness' into those who are to be saved. Rather, it consists in 'pardoning their sins' and in 'accounting and accepting their persons as righteous'.

Here we note at the outset that they distinguish justification from sanctification, which (in a subsequent chapter) they define in terms of God's creating 'a new heart and a new spirit' in the subjects of God's saving grace.

Justification is God's 'imputing the obedience and satisfaction of Christ' to someone. Nothing else has any merit but only Christ's work in life and death. Whilst it is true that the person justified exercises faith, yet neither their faith nor anything else, such as 'the act of believing' or 'other evangelical obedience', contributes merit in the least degree to the justified person. They are admitted into a justified state 'for Christ's sake alone'. Furthermore, the very faith by which they are justified is 'the gift of God'.

In their choice of expression the Westminster divines were scrupulously careful to exclude all possible forms of human merit.

The means by which a sinner receives Christ's righteousness is faith, which, they emphasise, is 'the alone instrument of justification'. It is to be noted that there is no place found in their doctrine of justification for the sacraments of baptism or the Lord's supper. Faith alone and without works, devotions or other virtues is the means by which the sinner enters into a state of being righteous before God.

However, faith here needs to be defined. There is such a thing as a 'dead faith'. By this they mean a purely nominal, or else intellectual faith, which is faith in name only. The faith which justifies, on the other hand, is 'not alone in the person justified, but is ever accompanied with all other saving graces'. It is 'no dead faith, but worketh by love'.

It is clear that this definition of 'faith' reflects the earlier conviction of these divines that the faith which justifies 'is the gift of God'. In explanation we can say that saving faith is the result of the new birth. Before anyone *can* exercise this saving faith he, or she, must be 'born again'. Hence, the faith which saves is not an act simply of the human will but is an expression of the new life of the soul now regenerated. It is in this sense that saving faith is 'the gift of God', as they put it.

The great question now to be answered is: Where did the righteousness come from by which the believer is justified? To explain this most central question they state: 'Christ, by his obedience and death, did fully discharge the debt of all those that are thus justified'.

The concept here is that Christ acted as the Representative of his people and discharged their obligations to God's justice by a perfect life and a cursed death on the cross. The Lord Jesus, in other words, was our Substitute and did for us by his life and death all that was necessary to instate his people in a right legal standing with God.

Their words are that Christ 'did make a proper, real and full satisfaction to his Father's justice in their behalf'. So great a mercy is to be put down only to God's 'free grace'. Nothing in us or done by us, whether before justification or after, contributes by the least degree of merit to our justified condition.

All the honour of our justification must be ascribed to God so that 'both the exact justice and rich grace of God might be glorified'.

The next aspect of justification taken up by the Westminster divines is: When are the people of God justified, in time or in eternity past? This question requires to be explained because it is clear from the teaching of Scripture that 'God did, from all eternity, decree to justify all the elect'. Since this is a Scripture truth, we must seek to know whether these elect persons are justified before they are actually brought to faith in this life or else justified when they come to faith.

34

The Confession affirms: 'they are not justified until the Holy Spirit doth, in due time, actually apply Christ to them'. That is, at the moment when they receive grace to believe savingly in Jesus Christ.

At the foundation of this definition is the wonderful truth of God's eternal election, by which he has of his own free will determined to choose some of Adam's race to eternal life and to pass by others so as to leave them to themselves and to the judgment which their sins deserve.

It is the certain teaching of Scripture that God has, before the world began, decided whom he will, and will not, save and justify.

When we consider how great our sins are and how great is our guiltiness before God, it is a matter of wonderment and profound gratitude that God has elected to save any. This teaching is necessary so that we might understand that, if we have come to a saving knowledge of God, it is only through the eternal choice of God and not for any merit in ourselves.

In a fifth paragraph the Confession looks at the pastoral aspects of this doctrine. Granted that our pre-conversion sins are pardoned in our justification, what is the way in which we should think of sins committed after conversion? 'God doth continue to forgive the sins of those that are justified'. However, sin is still sin in the lives of Christians. By our sins after conversion we 'may . . . fall under God's fatherly displeasure, and not have the light of his countenance restored unto' us until we humble ourselves, confess our sins, beg God's pardon and renew our 'faith and repentance'.

There is a price to pay if we sin after justification. However, mercifully, that price is never to be permitted by God to 'fall from the state of justification'. All who are justified will at last be glorified. But we dare not treat sin with impunity in this life of grace. If we fall into sin we must, like Peter, grieve for our sin and repent. But, like Peter, we have the comforting assurance that we shall not be cast away.

A final question is handled in the Westminster definition. Is there any difference between the way Old Testament believers were justified and the way in which New Testament believers are justified today? The view which these divines give is that there is no difference. Abraham, David, Daniel and all other Old Testament saints were justified by faith alone in the promise of God that a Saviour should one day come into the world. Obviously, we in our time know more of Christ and his glorious redemption than Old Testament saints did. But what knowledge they had was sufficient for them to believe and so be justified by the grace of God.

We have here the whole of what the Westminster divines state on this doctrine in their Chapter 11, 'Of Justification'. They emphasise that justification is to be had by faith alone. In that they endorse completely the conviction of Luther and the Reformers, and therefore differ fundamentally from the Roman Catholic view of justification.

We should notice also that there is in the above definition no attempt to bring in the concept of God's covenant, as is being done by modern writers who are of the New Perspective view. This modern view of course was not in mind at the time when the Confession was written, but the terms which they use make it clear enough that they viewed 'righteousness' as a forensic term.

8. The Healthy Fear of God

BEFORE we come to God for his pardon and justification we may expect to have fears and doubts. It is a common experience in those who come into a right relationship with God that, before they know the sweet relief of sins forgiven, they have a troubled conscience and a fight within their own heart. They are aware that God is displeased with them; yet they do not know how to escape.

The Bible shows us this in the case of several whom God is intending to bring to Christ and to bless with salvation. We see this in the life of Adam and Eve after they have sinned. When they 'heard the voice of the Lord God walking in the garden in the cool of the day' they 'hid themselves from the presence of the Lord God amongst the trees of the garden' (*Gen.* 3:8). A consciousness of sin made them afraid now to meet God, whom they inwardly knew they had disobeyed.

Some time prior to his meeting with Christ on the Damascus Road, Saul of Tarsus had an uneasy awareness that he had not kept the tenth commandment. He was still a proud Pharisee and unconverted but God began to shake his proud Pharisaism by means of this commandment. 'I was alive without the law once: but when the commandment came, sin revived, and I died' (*Rom.* 7:9). He is here explaining how his former self-confidence began to be disturbed. He was not now so confident in his own good standing before God as he had previously been.

The tenth commandment showed proud Saul of Tarsus that outward obedience to God's laws is not enough. God requires purity and holiness in our secret thoughts and desires. In this way the tenth commandment acted as a mirror to Saul. He saw himself now as God saw him: a sinner in spite of all his outward religiosity. He puts it like this: 'sin revived, and I died' (*Rom.* 7:9). In other words, he now came to realise the reality and guilt of his own sinful heart. As a consequence his proud opinion of himself received a mortal blow.

We refer to this and similar experiences in people, prior to their coming to Christ by faith, as 'law work'. By this expression we mean that God makes use of his law in our conscience in such a way that we become troubled about our spiritual condition.

This is necessary because sin has so ruined our soul that the conscience becomes sleepy and dead. Conscience is that faculty in the soul which God has placed there to rouse us to a sense of our guilt when we do wrong. We do not, as sinners, enjoy the sting of conscience when it pricks and smites us. But conscience is a good friend. Its work in the soul is very much for our profit.

When we read the conversion experiences of God's people, such as Martin Luther and John Bunyan, we see that it is this 'law work' which drove them to read the Bible, to pray and to seek God most earnestly. They at length came to know the peace of being justified through faith in Christ. But 'law work' was used by God to stir up their souls to cry out to him for light, mercy and grace.

One of the deepest reasons why some religious teachers have failed to understand and to define the doctrine of justification is that they have never experienced this 'law work'. They have probably never had their conscience roused to a realisation of what it is to be a sinner 'in the hands of an angry God'.

The fact is, that when the conscience is fully aroused, as was that of Luther and of Bunyan, there is only one thing that matters to a man or woman. They crave peace with God and forgiveness of sins. To get it they will abase themselves and cry to the Almighty with tears of anguish.

Their anxious desire is not just for church membership or for admittance into covenant privilege. It is above all else a craving for pardon and reconciliation with the God whose frown they are so acutely aware of. They come to an end of themselves. It is as if God places a coal from the fires of hell itself upon their conscience. So the Philippian gaoler felt when he cried out: 'What must I do to be saved?' (*Acts* 16:30). So did those who heard Peter's sermon on the Day of Pentecost feel when they 'were pierced in their heart' and anxiously asked, 'Men and brethren, what must we do?' (*Acts* 2:37).

When we are, as sinners, brought into this agonised state of soul, there is only one thing that can comfort us. We need to experience the peace of God which comes from being cleansed from all our sins by the blood of Christ. This is the experience of being justified. There is no relief sweeter than to be delivered from our sense of guilt and fear by the inward testimony of God's Holy Spirit that, being now fully cleansed and pardoned, we are the sons of God.

Whilst not all who become believing Christians have a dramatic conversion, some do. God's ways are different with each of his own dear people. But, whether dramatic or not, the experience of entering into a state of being justified with God is the most important and the most wonderful experience a person could ever have.

The fact that God takes stern means to bring his chosen people to himself in this world is a reminder to us that, were it not for his grace and love, none of us would ever repent and turn to him. God finds us all dead to what is heavenly and very much alive to the pleasures of this vain world. We speak of 'having to be cruel to be kind'. Similarly, God must needs shout loudly in our consciences to wake us up to our lost and condemned state. Only when we feel the weight of our guilt do we begin to seek God in earnest. It is for this reason that a famous Christian once said, 'I had been undone if I had not been undone'.

We are better placed now to understand what the Bible means when it tells us about God's 'call'.

This term is used a number of times in the New Testament to make it certain to us that it is God who takes the initiative always in bringing sinners into a state of justification. Of this fact we may not be conscious when we are first converted. It is common for a young believer to talk about his experience of conversion as though he himself took the initiative by making a decision to believe in Christ.

This is understandable in a newly-born child of God. His inner struggle and prayer for salvation are what he was most conscious of at the time of his conversion. He has possibly not had time yet to learn that before he himself began to seek after God there was a divine energy at work within his soul. This was the 'call' which led eventually to his coming to faith and repentance.

When we are better acquainted with the teaching of the Bible we are humbled to discover that all our searching for peace with God was the fruit of God's 'call' in our heart. This 'call' is given to men by God the Father and it is always effectual in those whom God is intending to bring to faith in Christ. Hence it is technically named the effectual calling ` of God. It is to be distinguished from the general summons to sinners which many hear through the lips of a faithful preacher of the gospel, but which they are able to ignore and to disregard. Jesus refers to this general 'call' in these words: 'Many are called, but few are chosen' (*Matt.* 22:14).

Of the many references in the New Testament we may for present purposes look at just this one: 'For whom he [God] did foreknow, he also did predestinate to be conformed to the image of his Son, that he might be the firstborn among many brethren. Moreover whom he did predestinate, them he also called: and whom he called, them he also justified: and whom he justified, them he also glorified' (*Rom.* 8:29, 30).

Here we see that the 'call' of God is an integral and essential element in the overall purpose of God in the salvation of his eternally-chosen people. The term 'foreknowledge' means that God in eternity past took a decision concerning them which would result in their being, in the course of their lifetime, brought into a state of justification. Further, it would result eventually in their glorification.

The 'call' is given, then, to all whom God has eternally chosen to salvation. They hear it in the course of their lifetime in this world, and they are by God constrained to answer the 'call' by giving themselves to him.

So the 'call' draws us to trust in Christ for salvation. That salvation comes to us as soon as we believe in Jesus Christ, for as soon as we believe we are justified.

9. Justification: the Way to Glory

GOD'S work is always perfect in conception, perfect in execution and perfect in completion. What he begins he will end. In this God is unique and to be praised. What men begin they may, or may not, finish. What they plan and prepare may look good on the drawing board but come to nothing in the end.

We use the word 'folly' to denote a building of any sort which some builder began but could not complete. Our Lord Jesus Christ uses this very thought in his preaching: 'Which of you, intending to build a tower, sitteth not down first . . .? lest haply, after he hath laid the foundation, and is not able to finish it, all that behold it begin to mock him' (*Luke* 14:28-29).

Thankfully God, being perfect in his wisdom, power and grace, never begins a work which he cannot finish. To our frail and imperfect understanding it might sometimes seem that the world has gone out of orbit and that history has no meaning, or no plan. In fact, the very reverse is true. God's eternal decrees and purposes are daily ripening and the day will come when every thought of his heart and mind will be brought to absolute and complete execution.

For the people of God this will bring unspeakable privileges of joy, comfort and love. All that ever happened to them will then be understood by his dear people as having 'worked together for good'. All life's trials and troubles were for our good.

Above all the Lord's people will wonder at the way in which their Lord and God has watched over them in all their wanderings in this uncertain world and steered them at last into the heavenly harbour, which they longed to see.

All whom God justifies shall at last be also glorified (*Rom.* 8:30). They will in the instant of their death cease to suffer or to sorrow any more. When a believer's soul leaves the body in

41

physical death, the soul is immediately in glory and in a state of perfection.

We refer to this as the Intermediate State of heaven. The soul is now morally perfect and can sin no more. But the believer is in a condition in which he is incomplete. He now rests in glory with all the saints who have gone before him and with all the angels, awaiting the great Last Day, when the trumpet shall sound and the bodies of all who have died will be raised up.

'In the twinkling of an eye' (*1 Cor.* 15:52) soul and body will come together again on that great day, the body being now raised in glory, and patterned after that of our glorified Saviour Jesus Christ.

All men must now appear at the throne of judgment on which Christ will sit to judge all who ever lived upon the earth. He will now separate mankind as a shepherd divides up his sheep from the goats. Those who have been in this life justified by faith in Christ will receive praise from Christ the Judge and will be welcomed into the glorious world of eternal happiness, the new heavens and new earth. There they will enjoy fellowship with the Triune God, Father, Son and Holy Spirit, to all eternity.

Those who in this life were never believers in Jesus Christ as their Saviour and so were never justified will, in the great Day of Judgment, be found guilty and unworthy to enter heaven. They shall, says Christ, be commanded by him in these solemn words: 'Depart from me, ye cursed, into everlasting fire, prepared for the devil and his angels' (*Matt.* 25:41).

It is to save us from so fearful a punishment that God sent his Son Jesus Christ into this world. The invitation of the gospel is to all who hear it: 'Believe on the Lord Jesus Christ and you will be saved.' This invitation is to all men, women and children everywhere. It is sent out to those in the West and to those in the East. It is sent out to those of the North and of the South. It is sent out to Jews and also to Gentiles: 'Whosoever will, let him take of the water of life freely' (*Rev.* 22:17). This 'water of life' is the sweet blessing of eternal salvation which Christ has purchased for sinners by his blood shed on the cross of Calvary.

To have this blessing a sinner needs nothing else but faith in Jesus as Saviour. This is so because God's promise cannot fail: 'Whosoever believeth in him shall not perish but have everlasting life' (*John* 3:16).

Is anything here in this life half so important then as this one thing: to be freely justified by God's grace?

For Further Reading

James Buchanan, *The Doctrine of Justification*, Banner of Truth Trust

John Owen, *The Doctrine of Justification by Faith*, vol. 5 of Owen's Collected Works, Banner of Truth Trust

Philip H. Eveson, *The Great Exchange*, Day One

R. C. Sproul, *Faith Alone*, Baker Books

William Cunningham, *Historical Theology*, vol. 2, Banner of Truth Trust

Thomas Goodwin, *Justifying Faith*, Works vol. 8, Banner of Truth Trust

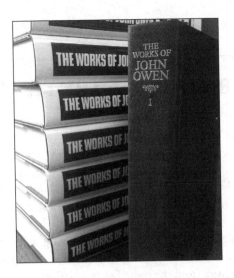

The Works of John Owen

Despite his other achievements, Owen is best famed for his writings. These cover the range of doctrinal, ecclesiastical and practical subjects. They are characterized by profundity, thoroughness and, consequently, authority. Andrew Thomson said that Owen 'makes you feel when he has reached the end of his subject, that he has also exhausted it.' Although many of his works were called forth by the particular needs of his own day they all have a uniform quality of timelessness. Owen's works were republished in full in the nineteenth century. Owen is surely the Prince of the Puritans. 'To master his works', says Spurgeon, 'is to be a profound theologian.'

16 volume set | clothbound | ISBN 978 0 85151 392 8

VOLUMES MAY ALSO BE PURCHASED INDIVIDUALLY

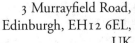